Forty Shades of Light in the Wilderness

by

Anthony Swaby

Grosvenor House
Publishing Limited

All rights reserved
Copyright © Anthony Swaby, 2021

The right of Anthony Swaby to be identified as the author of this
work has been asserted in accordance with Section 78
of the Copyright, Designs and Patents Act 1988

The book cover is copyright to Anthony Swaby

This book is published by
Grosvenor House Publishing Ltd
Link House
140 The Broadway, Tolworth, Surrey, KT6 7HT.
www.grosvenorhousepublishing.co.uk

This book is sold subject to the conditions that it shall not, by way of
trade or otherwise, be lent, resold, hired out or otherwise circulated
without the author's or publisher's prior consent in any form of binding or
cover other than that in which it is published and
without a similar condition including this condition being imposed
on the subsequent purchaser.

A CIP record for this book
is available from the British Library

ISBN 978-1-83975-481-4

Acknowledgements

Lois Swaby

Lois my wife has provided much inspiration and advice during this project. I would like to acknowledge and dedicate the success of this book to her. Thank you Lois.

***

Lyndsay Hill

Lyndsay has encouraged and supported me with advice from a proofreading angle. This has been an excellent foundation and springboard. Thank you Lyndsay.

Contents

1)	As we are gathered here	1
2)	As you arrived not as a King	2
3)	Between the two guilty bandits	3
4)	By my penitential nature	4
5)	He was not just an earthly man	5
6)	Help us to find within our Lenten journey	6
7)	Here around our sacred meeting	7
8)	Here within this building	8
9)	I am sad and lonely now	10
10)	I dedicate this place O Lord	11
11)	I have only found two options	12
12)	I heard the sounds disturb your peace	13
13)	I wash my hands O Lord	14
14)	If you are Lord Jesus Christ	15
15)	In the stillness of our prayers	17
16)	Jesus Christ my Lord and master	18
17)	Jesus Christ the comforter	19
18)	Lord Jesus Christ you are here again	21
19)	Mary the true disciple	22
20)	My chosen soul has turned to darkness	23
21)	My church was built on you	24
22)	My name is Caiaphas	25
23)	My real name is Gestas	26
24)	My sight was blinded from you Lord	27
25)	My weaknesses have caused the mistakes	28

26)	Our hearts of stone through your dear love	29
27)	Our Lord will ascend	30
28)	Peter your name is gracious	31
29)	The day they called me from my task	32
30)	The Jewish law has set my path	33
31)	The palms and cloaks before you Lord	34
32)	The route to Heaven's door has been reopened	35
33)	Through your eloquence Lord Jesus	36
34)	We felt your pain Lord Jesus Christ	37
35)	You came that day sat on a colt	38
36)	You have come Lord into these courts	39
37)	You have left an image within me	40
38)	You rode as prophets had foretold	41
39)	Your cross of pain and glory	42
40)	Your dear body now is resting	43

Introduction

I have written this book as a potential support for those who are thinking of either presenting a play or Sketch during the season of Lent, Holy Week or an event that symbolises either the season or character that is portrayed.

The book is split into fourteen chapters that have been called 'Shades'. Nine of the Shades are dedicated to characters like Mary, Peter, Judas and Joseph of Arimathea. In the Shades I have written a collection of poems that can be used to compliment a sketch or group of sketches and compliment the message of Holy Scripture and Biblical teaching.

The other five Shades are dedicated to Red Letter Days such as Ash Wednesday, Palm Sunday and Maundy Thursday. These again have been written to compliment or underline the importance of each day or time that is illustrated.

If you wish to use any of the poems within a group setting or include the poetry within your worship or teaching, each has a well=known that can be used and is familiar to most church musicians or praise bands.

It is my hope that it will be possible for you to use this book as an assistant and strengthen the message that is presented during Lent and Holy Week.

Anthony Swaby

Tunes

Abbots Leigh
By my penitential nature
Your dear body now is resting

Aurelia
Your cross of pain and glory

Austria
Through your eloquence Lord Jesus

Bishopsthorpe
He was not just an earthly man
I heard the sounds disturb your peace
Our hearts of stone through your dear love
He was not just an earthly man

Breslau
Lord Jesus Christ you are here again

Bunessan
The route to Heaven's door
has been reopened

Carlisle
The Jewish law has set my path

Camberwell
My name is Caiaphas

Contemplation
You came that day sat on a colt

Dix
In the stillness of our prayers

Dominus Regit Me
You have come Lord into my court
My real name is Gestas

Dulce Carmen
Here around our sacred meeting

Horsley
You rode as prophets had foretold

Hyfrydol
Your dear body now is resting

Jesus Our Redeemer
Here within this building

Knecht Kocher
Between the two guilty bandits

Liebster Jesu
I am sad and lonely now

Peter your name is gracious

Little Cornard
As we are gathered here

Love Divine
You have left an image within me

Londonderry Air
Help us to find within our Lenten journey

Maccabeus
Our Lord will ascend

Nun Danket
I wash my hands O Lord

Passion Chorale
Mary the true disciple

Praise My Soul
Jesus Christ my Lord and master
My weaknesses have caused the mistakes

Regent Square
My sight was blinded from you Lord

Richmond
As you arrived not as a King

Rockingham
I dedicate this place O Lord

St Cecilia
My church was built on you

St Gertrude
Jesus Christ the comforter
If you are Lord Jesus Christ

St Magnus
We felt your pain Lord Jesus Christ

Schmuchke Dich
My chosen soul has turned to darkness

Westminster Abbey
I have only found two options

Wiltshire
The palms and cloaks before you Lord

Woodlands
The day they called me from my task

As we are gathered here

As we are gathered here,
I solemnly declare.
Not all within this place,
will all your graces share.
Through legal acts of care and grace,
we will these people so embrace.

* * *

Not all will be transformed,
in body soul and core.
But ere through heavenly eyes,
the Lord is shown much more.
To nurture not the cross's blame,
but win salvation for the same.

* * *

So may the mission be,
for this anointed place.
To sow and root your Word,
displaying peace and grace.
Inspiring every soul to be
thus clothed to share your victory.

As you arrived not as a King

As you arrived not as a king,
but on a donkey bare.
Inspiring all who looked that way,
your servanthood to share.

* * *

Despite the sadness known to you,
that sad week should endure,
You faced each day with truth and hope,
that God alone could cure.

* * *

So as our lives sometimes face trials,
mid temptation and foe.
Then may we find your peace and strength,
to follow your path and grow.

Between the two guilty bandits

Between the two guilty bandits,
hung Jesus Christ our Lord.
Convicted and insulted,
by those he had adored.

* * *

Midst pain and true dejection,
that bitterness should bring.
We see the valour c;early,
of Heaven's most gracious king.

* * *

The third day was triumphant,
as from the tomb he rose.
Where kinsfolk ere did find there,
his folded linen clothes.

* * *

Where is the Lord my saviour?
was Mary's urgent plea.
Not knowing that the gardener,
was really truly thee.

* * *

So help us on our journey,
to feel your constant love.
Not in the Devil's trappings,
but poured from Heaven above.

By my penitential nature

By my penitential nature,
your words flowed from me that day.
Have you no real fear of God then,
or perhaps you feel another way?
Why are you not remonstrating,
can't you just now let it be?
He's not here for his bad actions,
But his love will set us free!

* * *

Through our misdirected actions,
we are now brought to this place.
But, let's face it for all our neighbours,
we bring nothing but shame and disgrace.
So though it's so late let's think on
and try very hard to calm down.
So even at this very sad moment,
true peace may win over from the frown.

* * *

Alas for our Lord is speaking,
at this most appointed time.
His tone is quietly directed,
at your heart and not your crime.
You still have a place beside me,
is what he has duly said.
Paradise is your real new bounty,
and the path he hopes you'll tread.

He was not just an earthly man

He was not just an earthly man,
of some unknown sad place,
Carrying calm peace, hope and love,
and kindled with God's grace.

* * *

Your gracious news has stirred us all,
and challenged some priests above.
Reminding us all to truly commit,
To your redeeming love.

* * *

You have a real presence from on high.
borne from the fore to the end,
Help us to find you, just as we are,
and count you as a true friend.

* * *

I'm just a soldier working through day,
and matching the pace of the rest,
Somehow today is taking its toll,
draining all and quite a long hard test.

* * *

Alas, Lord Jesus you've made me see,
the side of my work that's not fun.
As I reflect on all that's been shared,
maybe a convert has been won?

Help us to find within our Lenten journey

Help us to find within our Lenten Journey,
the measure of your sacrifice for all.
That did provide the price of true salvation,
and brought redemption when your Son did fall.
We pray that Christians in this Lenten journey,
will find the peace and glory you will being.
That on the day you bind us all together,
we may rejoice and there your blessed praises sing.

* * *

As we explore the treasures you have written,
within the pages of your Word of old.
Unveiling blessings through the generations,
that share the richness of your love foretold.
We pray that Christians on this Lenten Journey,
will find the peace and glory you will bring.
That on the day you bind us all together,
we may rejoice and there your blessed praises sing.

* * *

May we exchange your gems and inspirations,
that have occurred when we could see your face.
As sharing blessings freshly clothed with glory,
you transformed earth with your incarnate grace.
We pray that Christians on their Lenten journey,
will find the peace and glory you will bring.
That on the day you bind us all together,
we may rejoice and there your blessed praises sing.

Here around our sacred meeting

Here around our sacred meeting
your disciples met that night.
As you still revealed more clearly,
how to serve your neighbour right.
That the mission you ignited,
will remain within your sight.

* * *

Sometimes neighbours are distracted,
and feel tensions deep within.
Help us so to ease their burdens,
steering them away from sin.
That their lives may richly blossom,
as new souls they soon will win.

* * *

As your love so richly conquers,
and your kingdom here doth grow.
So equip us with your teaching,
through the Word that you did sow.
That within the Lenten season,
you will highlight what to know.

* * *

You have left us with a vision,
that was drawn from Heaven above.
Where our everlasting Father,
sent you down softer than dove.
To articulate on earth's soil,
grace and his redeeming love.

Here within this building

Here within this building,
shall we reverently rejoice.
Through a blend of praise and worship,
bonded in one voice.
Heralding the true king,
duly clothed in majesty.
Who through all times has forever,
claimed the victory.

* * *

Your son our redeemer,
destined for the skies above.
Illustrated how to witness,
your true heavenly love.
Heralding the true king,
duly clothed in majesty.
Who through all times has forever,
claimed the victory.

* * *

In our Lenten Journey,
we shall aim to see your face.
Though sometimes beyond clear vision,
bonded with your grace.
Heralding the true king,
duly clothed in majesty.
Who through all times has forever,
claimed the victory.

* * *

As we grasp your vision,
through our acts of praise and prayer.
Please unite our onward journey,
with your love so kind and fair.
Heralding the true king,
duly clothed in majesty.
Who for all times has forever,
claimed the victory.

I am sad and lonely now

I am sad and lonely now,
without you my friend and brother.
When I saw your final bow,
there seemed no route to recover.
As your Word becomes more clearer,
may my life be ever nearer.

* * *

As you hung upon the cross,
so my heart was filled with sorrow.
Not a sinner but a saint,
dying for your brethren's morrow.
As your friends denied ill-treated,
till your mission was completed.

* * *

When I came to you that morn,
to anoint your body bounded.
But the stone now had been moved,
as true Heavenly grace surrounded.
As you reign with God in glory,
help me so to tell your story..

* * *

Thank you for including me,
as a humble poor disciple.
Following the earthly path,
tracing Jesus Christ's full cycle.
Thanks for all your daily mission,
that inspires my new fruition.

I dedicate this place O Lord

I dedicate this place O Lord,
for your body cut down for me.
Your sacrifice was clearly shown,
to those who saw you on the tree.

* * *

I know the angels will protect,
this place until you move once more.
Till then may all who watch and pray,
be ever near their master's door.

* * *

For those who still now have to find,
the Lenten message you provide.
Our thoughts and prayers are lifted high,
that they will know you as their guide.

* * *

So now I leave you here in peace,
protected with the Spirit's love.
Inspired directed and redeemed.
with grace as gentle as the dove.

I have only found two options

I have only found two options,
set before me on this day.
If you would but answer clearly,
but you have nothing to say.
Therefore I am so restricted,
and dismiss your case this day.

* * *

Can you really build a kingdom,
in the space of three whole days.
As you have no stones or builders,
your project is a weird craze!
As when asked you remain silent,
please young sir take to your ways.

* * *

So perhaps the higher elders,
can assist your journey through.
With their reasoned legal vision,
oversee with a clearer view.
That your onward destination,
will bring out the best for you.

I heard the sounds disturb your peace

I heard the sounds disturb your peace,
lashings and cries were they.
Although I knew not this poor man,
his fate should not have come this way.

* * *

His followers have disowned him now,
though harnessed for many a year.
One said he was not from the same town,
another saw money far too dear.

* * *

Although this man was God's dear son,
at least that's what he said.
The title he had was 'King of the Jews'.
Inscribed above his head.

* * *

So this is all in one days work,
etched clearly in my mind.
Although I clearly have no faith,
find it hard to totally unwind.

I wash my hands O Lord

I wash my hands O lord,
as there is no decision.
Although wishing you well,
I fail to see your mission.
How can you really say...,
your kingdom soon to be.
In three days will be found,
until eternity.

***

I've heard many a case,
of people from all races.
But you alas dear Lord,
have no real airs or graces
So understand my plea,
of ignorance ere surpassed.
I fail to really see,
the vision you have grasped.

***

Maybe your earthly work,
will one day be exalted.
As Christian folk grow strong,
and sinful wrongs are faulted?
But now I clearly see,
For you as man and friend.
There's no more I can do
than say this is the end.

If you are Lord Jesus Christ

If you are Lord Jesus Christ,
called the Son of God.
Why are you still walking,
where normal folk trod
If your heavenly father,
has anointed you?
Why are you before me,
and what can I do?

* * *

Refrain

Why don't you give answer
to the simple plea.
I will then release you,
if your case I see.

* * *

Please tell us why you are mute.
here within this court.
Other folk have told us,
many you have taught.
Through your teachings and mission.
here within this land.
But you simply fail to answer,
as you face the stand

Refrain

* * *

Though I wish to help you more,
you give me no choice.
As you fail to help me,
through no active voice.
Please help us to help you
and assist us more.
Otherwise your freedom,
will be just a flaw!

In the stillness of our prayers

In the stillness of our prayers
may we hear your voice so true.
That reflects your Word so clearly,
guiding us in all we do.
That our lives may always share,
loving wisdom peace and care.

* * *

As we read through every page,
that unfolds your wisest sight.
Sharing that you'll always be,
our Messiah born to fight.
That our lives will always share,
loving wisdom peace and care.

* * *

As you so prepare our lives,
with your grace so freely found.
May we grasp your Holy mind,
transformed, brightened and unbound.
That our lives will always share,
loving wisdom peace and care.

Jesus Christ my Lord and master

Jesus Christ my Lord and master,
now you're here what do you bring?
Peace for all folk of the nations,
and to end their suffering?
Can you answer my small question,
how did you become a king?

* * *

If you are the son of God then,
why is he not here with you?
Or perhaps through his wise vision,
he knows faith will see you through.
Trusting that the best will follow
everything that you will do.

* * *

So then Jesus please now help us,
as we aim to meet your need.
And although we want to reach you,
here we're stuck with laws indeed.
So again I ask you clearly,
dear Lord Jesus what's your plea?

Jesus Christ the comforter

Jesus Christ the comforter,
came from Heaven above.
With his father's blessing,
clothed in Heavenly love.
To redeem the nations,
to the end of time.
Circled with salvation,
perfect and sublime.

* * *

Refrain

*Jesus draw us closer,
through our praise and prayer.
That we may find new strength,
as the Devil we stare!*

* * *

He alone translated,
through his love divine.
Through his many teachings,
as radiance did shine.
As he glows so brightly,
during Passiontide.
May our love grow richly,
bursting out with pride.

Refrain

* * *

As our lives promote thee,
in our work and praise.
May our neighbours see more,
through our Christ like ways.
That our lives reflected,
may complete the prize.
That was clearly glorious,
when you did arise.

Refrain

Lord Jesus Christ you are here again

Lord Jesus you are here again,
the second time within a week.
Please tell me have you changed your plea?
or are you still bewildered and bleak?

* * *

You know these courts have legal lines,
that offer statutes firm and true.
Within that guise I can advise,
that's sadly not good news for you.

* * *

However Lord please let us know
what happened at the previous place,
With that we may discern and know,
how we can now improve your case.

Mary the true disciple

Mary the true disciple,
followed right to the end.
And saw the crucifixion,
of her very best friend.
With sadness and reluctance,
saw the courts duly frame.
A guilty hardened bandit,
freed of a shameful blame.

* * *

Seeking her dear Lord Jesus,
upon the break of day.
Finding the tomb was opened,
and cloths where he had lay.
Not knowing that the gardener,
was her disguised Lord.
Found the new revelation,
had struck a fresh new chord.

* * *

So can we find this season,
amidst readings and prayer.
The heartbeat of this Lenten,
through peace and loving care.
Showing us all the real truth,
much softer than a dove.
Destined for all our neighbours,
anointed with your love.

My chosen soul has turned to darkness

My chosen soul turned to darkness,
when temptation brought real sadness.
Not through honesty of being,
but with misdirected thieving.
As the silver pieces pointed,
to a treasure not anointed
But clothed with guilt and sighing,
as my darkened life is dying.

* * *

All my guilty saddened features,
have revealed my hidden creatures.
That for many years were hidden,
although only half forbidden.
Now with true image revealed,
as my hidden faith once healed.
Now though stained and duly blighted,
needs to be spiritually righted

My church was built on you

My church was built on you,
as your faith ere so strong.
Would build a platform new,
and keep alive my song.

***

Your promise bold and true,
when taken from the shore.
By showing lame and free,
the joys at Heaven's door

***

Across the years your catch,
of folk would burst all nets.
And many would have said,
you caused no real regrets.

***

Until in the last days,
before the cock did crow
You thrice denied our bond,
and claimed you did not know.

***

So in our Lenten path,
please help us Lord to know.
How to affirm our vows,
and daily like you grow.

My name is Caiaphas

My name is Caiaphas,
born and bred a Jew.
Nurtured in legal statutes,
that all people should pursue.
With a High Priest's guidance,
Annus was his name.
I learned how to do no more,
but be the same.

***

In the Gospel message,
as St John so states.
Anna brings the Lord Jesus,
right before my office gates.
There Peter denied me,
declaring not to know.
The bond that between us,
helped your kingdom grow.

My real name is Gestas

My real name is Gestas,
or a bad thief
Crucified with Jesus,
noted for my grief.
Jesus Christ the saviour,
saved so many folk.
But at the last moments,
he bore his yoke.

* * *

I heard you were a prince,
born to be a king.
But you seem like us folk,
with no more to bring.
The high courts and Pilate,
could your charges see,
And your voice was silent,
when they sought your plea.

* * *

As the clock struck noontime,
and the skies went black.
So the Heavens opened,
with a thunderous crack.
Then some folk saw clearly,
your redeeming grace.
As your link with Heaven,
came right to this place.

My sight was blinded from you Lord

My sight was blinded from you Lord,
by the darkness of my sin.
And my strength has truly vanished.
as the devil tries hard to win.
May this Lenten pathway lead me,
to restore my soul within.

* * *

As I seek to follow duly,
help me now your way to know.
That restored to former glories,
I may with your blessings grow.
That this Lenten pathway leads me
to embrace your radiant glow.

* * *

As the Easter season beckons,
with your resurrection clear.
Pointing to your Father's union,
that seems far but is always near.
May the Lenten pathway lead me,
how to make your message clear.

* * *

So dear brother as your servant,
please make clear my mission's view.
That my new renewed direction,
is always alongside you!
That the Lenten pathway leads me,
in everything I say and do.

My weaknesses have caused the mistakes

My weaknesses have caused the mistakes,
that destroyed my life I had.
Following our dear Lord Jesus,
and supporting the lame and sad.
But through my weakness of service,
everything has turned out bad.

* * *

Over three years I heard your words,
of correction, hope and praise,
Sharing your devoted vision,
with your calm constructive ways.
But my failure at the climax,
severed my disciple's days.

* * *

When attending your last supper,
you encouraged us to know.
That we all should love each other,
through making your true love show.
And explaining how to nurture
a new being that should flow.

* * *

But my weaknesses were greater,
than your nurtured love within.
That my mind, heart. and new witness,
was now drowning deep in sin.
So as a disgraced disciple,
meant that I was not your kin.

Our hearts of stone through your dear love

Our hearts of stone through your dear love,
are transformed from within.
Displaying your grace and holiness,
and purified from sin.

* * *

The transformation ere begins,
the day we turn to thee.
And walk beneath the radiant light,
that guides the path we see.

* * *

As every candle burns a flame,
relating to folk of yore.
Help us to find within us this day,
the courage to love you more.

* * *

Mary's obedience clearly shows,
the bond she shared and knew.
Revealing how to serve the Lord,
and deepen the things we do.

* * *

So shall we walk this Lenten path,
observing your life of old.
Embracing how to steward your earth,
and be gathered within one fold.

Our Lord will ascend

Refrain

Our Lord will ascend,
high above the sky.
To redeem his people,
from his throne on high.

* * *

Where with God and Spirit,
as the Trinity.
You have made a stronghold.
with the angels be.

Refrain

Lord you sent your Son down,
to this earthly place.
There to give your image,
through heavenly grace.

Refrain

Lent now shows us how through,
Peter's loosened jaw.
And a sad denial,
death could be no more

Refrain

May you help our footsteps,
so to track your line.
That your Easter glories,
in our lives may shine.

Peter your name is gracious

Peter your name is gracious,
a platform so mighty and bold.
Inspired and just held high,
sought and respected by the fold.
Yet are you so still to falter,
as your back turned to the altar.

***

Till then you followed Jesus,
when from the boat you came brightly.
Teaching the faith so boldly,
to turn those who failed uprightly
But was the unseen armour failing,
as the tests were too prevailing.

***

Alas with our earthly path.
we are let to know your rigour.
Through the difficulties and trials,
when we find you in our vigour.
So within our Lenten glory,
shall we tell the glorious story.

The day they called me from my task

The day you called me from my daily task,
asking of me to fish for only you.
Although I really did not have a grasp,
it clearly was the right thing to pursue.

* * *

Over the years your hand has stretched right out,
and healed the damaged parts of every mind.
Through loving wisdom seamless care for all,
restoring truth and peace to humankind.

* * *

You built a church around my name good Lord,
saluting my strengths boldness as the flair.
Maintaining clearly that true faith would grow,
for all the people in my pastoral care.

* * *

Although you offered me so much I failed,
resisting your due calling from my core.
As when I needed to stand out and serve,
my courage failed as I knew you no more.

The Jewish law has set my path

The Jewish law has set my path,
drawing from historic time.
To discern if you can be set free,
or punished for the crime.

***

After the questions that you were asked,
no answers were offered that were complete.
Not giving us a strong line to proceed,
But leading sadly to your defeat.

***

Jesus the system is out of our hands,
despite the bold efforts we have made.
Maybe the courts now will duly reveal,
a verdict for you that will never fade.

The palms and cloaks before you Lord

The palms and cloaks before you Lord,
were blessed from Heaven above.
To illustrate the sacrifice,
of your undying love.

* * *

Each step the donkey trod that day,
was punctuated grace.
As you were carried triumphantly,
to the appointed place.

* * *

As we now dedicate our lives,
into this Holy Week.
Encourage us to love you more,
as we your face doth seek.

The route to Heaven's door has been reopened

The route to Heaven's door has been reopened,
as the world's darkness now turns to light.
As we await your flickers of brightness,
so may our new lives be truly bright.

***

In this our vigil may we see clearly,
how you have renewed our mission here.
That we may truly work with our neighbours,
bonding our skills to make your Word clear.

***

Within our prayers we remember duly,
all those who need your fatherly care.
Thanking you for their talents and treasures,
and for the love and graces we share.

***

So Lord we look forward to the dawning,
and we await your radiance divine.
When we may firmly and truly greet thee,
stepping to boldly make your light shine!

Through your eloquence Lord Jesus

Through your eloquence Lord Jesus
you have been a shining star.
As the varied folk come searching,
you accept them as they are.
Now you're midst a situation,
that requires a balanced view.
So I need to think more clearly,
as I reason what to do.

* * *

Never have I had a person,
who is titled as a king.
And does not command a nation,
but speaks of the peace he can bring.
Where am I to start my thinking.
and be fair in legal eyes.
By releasing I'll be slaughtered.
otherwise I have no prize.

* * *

So I find myself imprisoned,
stuck in an impossible yoke.
As a loyal male professional,
this is certainly no joke.
But alas I'll pass it over,
to Pilate for his wise view.
Then he'll have time to consider,
and direct the next way through.

We felt your pain Lord Jesus Christ

We felt your pain Lord Jesus Christ,
through cruel nails and spear.
And know how many failed their task,
although they claimed to hear.

* * *

Your teaching though clear and precise,
to those you trained and knew.
But Simon did reject thee thrice,
claiming he knew not you.

* * *

The strong temptation of the coins,
forced Judas so to turn.
And with the signal of a kiss,
thwarted what he did learn.

* * *

So help us Lord this day to know,
the role that lies therein.
Protecting and revealing how,
to keep our souls from sin.

You came that day sat on a colt

You came that day sat on a colt,
a calm and glorious ride.
With dignity and purposeful steps,
revealing peace and pride.

* * *

The palms and cloaks that paved the way,
were laid by those who care.
To mark the ministry you gave,
along with healing prayer.

* * *

Your heavenly grace has always been,
a seal with God above.
An ere united partnership,
that magnifies true love.

* * *

Now as we walk along your path,
seeking to know you more.
So may your light reveal the route,
that leads us to your door.

You have come Lord into these courts

You have come lord into these courts,
your case not so attracting.
With nothing but true faith with hope,
and God's divine reacting.

* * *

The laws we have are so entwined
with deeply rooted history.
The blasphemy and guilt you hold.
is not the route to victory.

* * *

And so as I can do no more,
please take him from my vision,
For others to decide his new path,
that may restore his mission.

You have left an image within me

You have left an image in me,
that will stay until I die.
Etching how to serve your neighbour,
through the love of God on high.

* * *

You have given me a virtue,
that wipes out a selfish view.
Making sure that every person,
is to be considered too.

* * *

By this image all are equal,
with nobody up too high.
Till we meet you when we die.
with our eyes on heaven's sky.

You rode as prophets had foretold

You rode as prophets had foretold,
through Zechariah's sight.
To show your kingship to the world,
revealed with a great light.

* * *

The mode of transport did unfold,
you were the mighty king.
As many scholars had confirmed,
you alone peace could bring.

* * *

The cloaks and branches did express,
historic shouts of praise.
That on that day did ere resound,
your true angelic ways.

Your cross of pain and glory

Your cross of pain and glory,
beneath the mid day sky.
Was shrouded in the darkness,
as God reached from on high.
To there respect your witness,
of teaching, pain and joy.
Concluding as was destined,
for you both man and boy.

* * *

The loneliness of grieving,
that you were forced to face.
For misdirected reasons,
was surely a disgrace.
But through real dedication,
and pureness of the heart.
The darkness of Good Friday,
has brought a fresh new start.

* * *

So let us now with vigour,
renew our Lenten sight.
Revising our transgressions,
to keep the vision right.
As we approach this Easter,
so may we know you more.
And reach out to our neighbours,
as we your face adore.

Your dear body now is resting

Your dear body now is resting,
within this meek hallowed place.
Away from more brutal damage,
sealed with heavenly peace and grace.
I have seen how God had spoken,
through your earthly mission done.
And in peace you rest securely,
a new era has begun.

* * *

Holy week has seen your passion,
clearly shown before us all.
As you dearly witnessed to us,
the true reason for your call.
So please help us now to deepen,
the faith you have clearly taught.
That we may so fashion always,
the grace that from Heaven you brought.

* * *

The darkness that ere surrounds us,
has now turned into new light.
If we now shall fight the devil,
and then steer toward the right.
Alas now we look towards you,
seeking your anointed face.
That we may so conquer boldly,
and transform this darkened place.

.

Shade One

Ash Wednesday

Help Us to Find Within Our Lenten Journey
In the Stillness of Our Prayers
Our Hearts of Stone Through Your Dear Love

Shade Two

Caiaphas

My Name Is Caiaphas
The Jewish Law Has Set My Path
You Have Come Lord Into These Courts

Shade Three

Good Friday

Between the Two Guilty Bandits
We Felt Your Pain Lord Jesus Christ
Your Cross of Pain and Glory

Shade Four

Herod

As We Are Gathered Here
I Have Only Found Two Options
Through Your Eloquence Lord Jesus

Shade Five

Holy Saturday

Jesus Christ the Comforter
Our Lord Will Ascend
The Route to Heaven's Door Has Been Reopened

Shade Six

Joseph of Arimathea

I Dedicate This Place O Lord
Jesus Christ My Lord and Master
Your Dear Body Now is Resting

Shade Seven

Judas

My Chosen Soul Has Turned to Darkness
My Sight Was Blinded from You Lord
My Weaknesses Have Caused the Mistakes

Shade Eight

Mary

I am Sad and Lonely Now
Mary the True Disciple
You Have Left an Image Within Me

Shade Nine

Maundy Thursday

As You Arrived Not as a King
Here Around Our Sacred Meeting
Here Within This Building

Shade Ten

Palm Sunday

The Palms and Cloaks Before You Lord
You Came That Day Sat on A Colt
You Rode as Prophets Had Foretold

Shade Eleven

Peter

My Church Was Built on You
Peter Your Name is Gracious
The Day They Called Me from My Task

Shade Twelve

Pilate

I Wash My Hands O Lord
If You Are Jesus Christ
Lord Jesus You Are Here Again

Shade Thirteen

Robbers

By My Penitential Nature
My Real Name Is Gestas

Shade Fourteen

Soldiers

He Was Not Just an Earthly Man
I Heard the Sounds Disturb Your Peace

About the Author

Anthony grew up in London and went to secondary school near Banbury in Oxfordshire. Whilst at school he sung in a choir and played piano as a soloist. Anthony was also voted as the most improved musician in his final year. Four years after school Anthony wrote some poems with ethical and moral leaning. Some of these were set to popular and original music.

In 1992 Anthony was ordained. A few years later was a member of the diocesan liturgical committee. Since then he has written various poems and songs for church settings and choirs and been encouraged to bring some of them together for various events with his friends and colleagues. It was this that ultimately encouraged Anthony to write *Rainbow of Anthology* in 2018. The pandemic of 2020 has encouraged Anthony to write *40 Shades of Light in the Wilderness*.

In his spart time Anthony enjoys walking, cricket, rugby, football and landscape photography.

Anthony is a full-time hospital chaplain in the West Midlands.

www.ingramcontent.com/pod-product-compliance
Lightning Source LLC
Chambersburg PA
CBHW031426040426
42444CB00006B/709